JS97.53
S756m

Food Webs

S0-BAH-689

Mountain Food Chains

WILDER BRANCH LIBRARY
7140 E. SEVEN MILE RD.
DETROIT, MI 48234

Louise and Richard Spilsbury

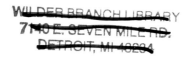

Heinemann Library
Chicago, Illinois

JAN 2006

WI

Chicago, Illinois

Customer Service   888–454–2279

Visit our website at www.heinemannlibrary.com

All rights reserved. No part of this publication may be reproduced or transmitted in any form or by any means, electronic or mechanical, including photocopying, recording, taping, or any information storage and retrieval system, without permission in writing from the publisher.

Photo research by Ruth Blair and Ginny Stroud-Lewis
Designed by Jo Hinton-Malivoire and AMR
Printed in China by WKT Company Limited.

09 08 07 06 05
10 9 8 7 6 5 4 3 2 1

Library of Congress Cataloging-in-Publication Data
Spilsbury, Louise.
  Mountain food chains / Louise Spilsbury and Richard Spilsbury.
     v. cm. -- (Food webs)
  Includes bibliographical references (p.   ).
  Contents: What is a mountain food web? -- What is a mountain food chain? -- What is a producer? -- What is a primary consumer? -- What is a secondary consumer? -- How are mountain food chains different in different places? -- What happens to a food web when a food chain breaks down? -- How can we protect mountain habitats and food chains?
  ISBN 1-4034-5856-1 (lib. bdg.) -- ISBN 1-4034-5863-4 (pbk.)
 1. Mountain ecology--Juvenile literature. 2. Food chains (Ecology)--Juvenile literature. [1. Mountain ecology. 2. Food chains (Ecology) 3. Ecology.] I. Spilsbury, Richard. II. Title. III. Series.
  QH541.5.M65S65 2004
  577.5'3--dc22
                              2003026195

Acknowledgments
The author and publisher are grateful to the following for permission to reproduce copyright material: Alamy p. **22**; a-z botanicals p. **17**; Corbis pp. **5** (David Muench), **7** (John M Roberts), **8**, **14**, **16** (Tom Brakefield), **10** (Galen Rowell), **15** (Gallo Images), **23** (Josef Polleross), **25** (John Van Hasselt), pp. **11**, **24**; Getty Images p. **27**; Heather Angel/Natural visions p. **12**; Nature PL pp. **13** (David Kjaer), **18** (Andrew Parkinson); Photodisk/Getty images p. **26**.

Cover photograph of a mountain hare eating red berries in the snow reproduced with permission of NHPA.

Illustrations by Words and Publications.

The publisher would like to thank Dr Dennis Radabaugh of the Department of Zoology at Ohio Wesleyan University for his comments in the preparation of this book.

Every effort has been made to contact copyright holders of any material reproduced in this book. Any omissions will be rectified in subsequent printings if notice is given to the publisher.

Contents

Some words are shown in bold, **like this**. You can find out
what they mean by looking in the glossary.

What Is a Mountain Food Web?

Just as in all **habitats**, plants and animals that live and grow in a mountain habitat depend on each other for food. This is because all **organisms** eat or are eaten by other organisms. For example, in a mountain habitat, rabbits eat grass and then may be eaten by eagles or foxes. When plants and animals die and rot, they are eaten by other living things, such as insects, **fungi**, and **bacteria**.

If you draw lines between the organisms in a habitat that eat each other, you create a diagram called a food web. It is called a web because it looks rather like a tangled spider's web! In food web diagrams, the arrows lead from the food to the animal that eats it.

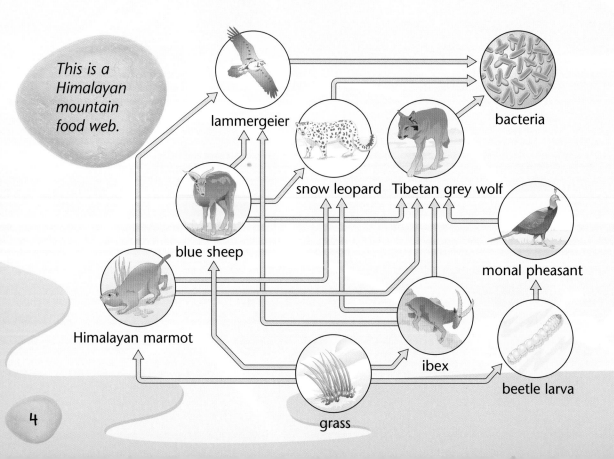

This is a Himalayan mountain food web.

lammergeier

bacteria

snow leopard

Tibetan grey wolf

blue sheep

monal pheasant

Himalayan marmot

ibex

beetle larva

grass

These are rhododendrons, growing in the Black Mountains of the eastern United States. These bushy plants with large flowers live in different mountain areas of the world.

What are mountain habitats like?

Mountains are areas of land that are over 1,640 feet (500 meters) high. They are steeper and much higher than hills. Mountains are found all over the world. Even in warm countries, mountains can have snowy peaks because temperatures drop as you get higher in the air. Plants and animals that live in mountain habitats have to be well-suited to life on the steep rocky slopes, with the harsh sunlight, fierce cold, and strong winds found there.

All the organisms that live in mountain areas are part of a mountain food web. Some, such as mountain rabbits and hares, live there all year round. Others, such as hummingbirds or American redstarts, visit mountains at certain times of year when there is plenty of food that they like to eat.

What Is a Mountain Food Chain?

Food webs are made up of many simpler food chains. Food chain diagrams show **organisms** that eat each other as links in a single chain. They follow the movement of food and **energy** from one link to another. The arrows in a food chain diagram show the direction that the energy moves.

Most plants and animals are part of more than one food chain because they eat or are eaten by more than one kind of organism. Animals that eat different kinds of food usually have a greater chance of survival than those that rely on just one kind of food. If an animal relied on one food source and that food supply ran out, the animal would starve.

This diagram of a mountain food chain shows how energy passes from one link in the chain to another.

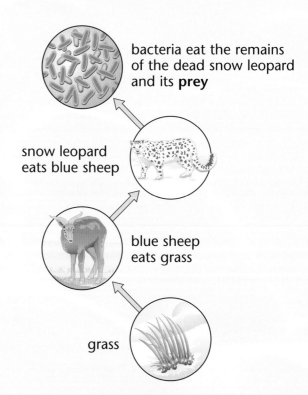

bacteria eat the remains of the dead snow leopard and its **prey**

snow leopard eats blue sheep

blue sheep eats grass

grass

*The plants in a mountain **habitat** are an important source of energy for all other organisms that live there. Only plants can trap energy from sunlight.*

Starting the chain

The Sun is the source of energy for almost all the living things on Earth. Plants are able to capture some energy from sunlight in their leaves. They use it to make their own food from water and a gas in the air called carbon dioxide, in a process called **photosynthesis**.

Besides food, plants need small amounts of **nutrients** from the soil. They take in these nutrients, along with water, through their roots.

Animals cannot get energy from the Sun—they get their energy from food. When animals eat plants, they gain some of the energy stored inside them. For example, mountain hares eat grass and birds eat tree berries. **Decomposers**, such as **fungi** and **bacteria**, get energy from feeding on dead plants and animals.

Making the chain

A food chain starts with a **producer**. Plants are known as producers because they make, or produce, food. Animals are **consumers**. They cannot make their own food. They have to eat plants or other **organisms** to get the **energy** they need to survive.

Herbivores are animals that feed mainly on plant parts, such as leaves, seeds, or berries. In food chains, herbivores are **primary consumers**—they are the first ones to gain energy from the plants they eat. **Carnivores**, animals that feed on other animals, are known as **secondary consumers**. They get energy from the animals they eat. Some animals called **omnivores** eat both plants and other animals. Omnivores can be both primary and secondary consumers.

The mountain lion is a carnivore, or secondary consumer. It often eats herbivores like this snowshoe hare.

More links in the chain

Food chains do not end when organisms eventually die. Animals called **scavengers** eat the dead remains of other animals. In mountain **habitats**, scavengers can be large, like vultures, or small, like worms or insects. **Decomposers** such as **bacteria** and **fungi** eat any dead remains not taken by scavengers. Decomposers break the remains into tiny pieces. Some pieces become food for the decomposers. Other pieces get washed into the soil and become **nutrients** for plants. When new plants take in these nutrients through their roots and use them to grow, the food chain begins again!

This diagram shows the movement of energy in a mountain food chain, from plant producer to primary consumer, and on to the secondary consumer and decomposer.

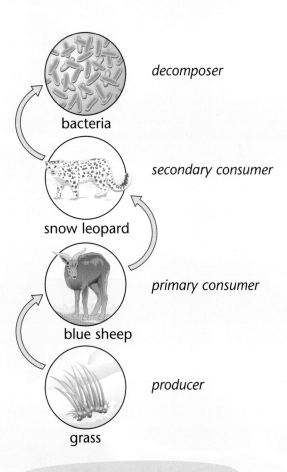

decomposer

bacteria

secondary consumer

snow leopard

primary consumer

blue sheep

producer

grass

Scavengers and decomposers have reduced this blue sheep to little more than bones.

Breaking the chain

All of the **organisms** in a food web are connected to each other and to their **habitat**. If some of the organisms die out, it may cause problems for others in their food web.

Sometimes natural events can damage a habitat and the food webs that exist within it. In an avalanche, large amounts of snow, ice, and rock slip down a mountain. An avalanche can knock down large areas of forest on the mountainside, destroying the habitat for many animals and plants. However, it also creates open areas that other **species** can use until the trees grow back. Human activity, such as taking over mountain land for buildings, can also cause breaks in mountain food chains and webs. When people disturb wild habitats and create **pollution**, some of the organisms within the habitat may die.

Which Producers Live in Mountains?

On mountains, as in all other habitats on Earth, plants are the **producers**. Different kinds of producers live at different heights on mountains. Lower slopes, where it is usually warmer and less windy, may have dense rain forests or areas of broad-leaved trees. Higher slopes often have trees with thin needles, such as pine and spruce. These trees can survive in colder temperatures.

At a certain point up a high mountain, it becomes too cold and windy for trees to grow. Above this **tree line**, tough, low-growing plants such as certain shrubs and grasses thrive. The highest parts of some mountains look like rocky wasteland. Most of the small plants here grow in sheltered gaps between rocks. One group of especially tough **fungi** called **lichens** live on bare rock faces. Lichens have tiny plantlike organisms called algae living inside them. In return for shelter, the algae produce food for the fungi!

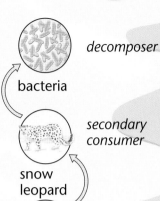
decomposer
bacteria

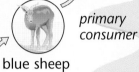
secondary consumer
snow leopard

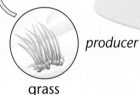
primary consumer
blue sheep

producer
grass

Can you see the tree line on this mountain?

11

This colorful flowering plant grows high in the Himalayan mountains. Many mountain flowering plants grow in sheltered spots, protected from the cold and wind by the surrounding rock.

Mountain flowers

Many flowering mountain plants grow close to the ground, out of the path of icy winds. Some have fine hairlike strands on their leaves and stems to trap a layer of warm air around them. They often have very colorful, highly scented flowers. These attract the few **pollinators**, such as bumblebees, that fly in mountain areas. In **temperate** areas, many flowering plants survive the cold winters underground as seeds or bulbs. They grow again in spring and summer. In higher, colder mountain regions, summers are very short. Plants grow, flower, and make their seeds in just two or three months.

Breaking the Chain: Producers

Trees are an important part of many mountain food chains. In the Andes Mountains of South America, the seeds of Polylepis trees are the main food of Cochabamba mountain finches. People chop down Polylepis trees for firewood. With fewer seeds to eat, the finches are getting rarer—there are just 2,500 adults left. **Predators** that eat the finches, such as falcons, then have less **prey** to eat.

Which Primary Consumers Live in Mountains?

Mountain **primary consumers** eat many different kinds of plants. Some are more picky than others. Bighorn sheep in the United States eat anything from grass and bark to moss, while Chinese giant pandas eat only particular kinds of bamboo. Small mountain **herbivores** may eat different parts of plants. Mountain pine beetle **larvae** live under pine tree bark and feed on sweet sap in the wood. Hummingbirds, bees, and moths fly from flower to flower in search of sweet nectar or **pollen** to eat.

Large mountain herbivores

Some mountain primary consumers are large **mammals**. Mountain zebras in southwestern Africa eat grass. They may spend half of each day grazing, to get the **energy** they need from the plants they eat. Mountain gorillas eat about 40 different kinds of plants, including vines, thistles, and wild celery.

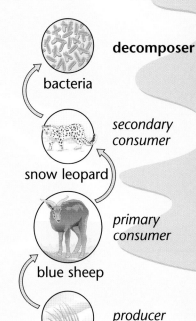

decomposer
bacteria

secondary consumer
snow leopard

primary consumer
blue sheep

producer
grass

Mountain birds such as grouse live on the ground and feed mostly on pine needles and berries from shrubs.

Mountain goats and hares

Mountain **mammals** usually have thick fur to protect them from the cold and wind as they search for food. Mountain goats have woolly hair for warmth. Their tough hooves protect their feet as they climb over hard rock cliffs looking for plant twigs and moss to eat. Mountain hares grow white fur in winter so **predators** cannot see them as easily against the snow. They can search more safely for grass or leaves to eat.

Mountain rodents

Many mountain **primary consumers**, such as pikas and marmots, are **rodents** that live underground and come out to feed. In autumn, pikas collect leaves and spread them out to dry before piling them in their holes, or burrows. Dry leaves survive the winter better than wet leaves, so their food stores last longer.

*Marmots spend most of the year eating the leaves and flowers of many different plants and grasses. They **hibernate** in winter when food is scarce.*

Which Secondary Consumers Live in Mountains?

Secondary consumers are animals that get their **energy** by eating other animals. Some are predators that chase and catch **prey** in mountain **habitats**. Others are **scavengers** that feed on dead animals.

Mountain birds of prey

Birds of prey are birds that hunt other animals to eat. They can soar over all levels of a mountain searching for food. Peregrine falcons and eagles hunt for birds in the sky and small **mammals** on the ground. Some birds, such as vultures and condors, are scavengers. Their wide wings allow them to soar on the breezes blowing up the sides of mountains as they look for dead animals.

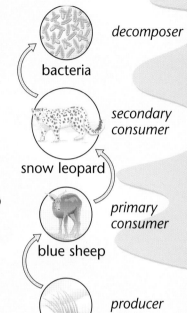

decomposer
bacteria

secondary consumer
snow leopard

primary consumer
blue sheep

producer
grass

The lammergeier is a mountain scavenger that often feeds on mammal skeletons. It carries bones up and drops them onto rocks to get at the juicy, jellylike marrow inside.

Mountain cats and dogs

The snow leopard is a rare mountain cat that hunts wild sheep and goats, marmots, hares, and birds. The mountain lion, also known as a cougar or puma, is another type of cat. It measures about six feet (two meters) long, and it eats large **mammals** such as deer and wild pigs. Some members of the dog family, such as foxes and coyotes, also live and feed on mountains. Both hunt mainly rabbits, hares, and **rodents**, but may also act as **scavengers**, by eating dead animals.

*Coyotes usually hunt alone for small **prey** like this mouse, but they sometimes hunt larger prey in packs.*

Breaking the Chain: Secondary Consumers

In parts of western North America where people have killed wolves, elk have increased in number because they have no **predators**. The elk then eat many plants from the edges of mountain rivers, reducing the shady areas where some kinds of fish feed and take shelter. In this way, killing the wolves also reduced the number of fish.

Which Decomposers Live in Mountains?

Decomposers are living things that feed on the remains of other organisms. Dead animals and plants and their wastes rot because decomposers break them down. When these remains rot, nutrients are released. Decomposers take in some of the nutrients, but others are released into the soil. Trees and other plants can take in these nutrients through their roots and use them to grow. Then they start new food chains and webs. Mountain decomposers include fungi and bacteria. Many live in the soil or under the shelter of rocks or plants.

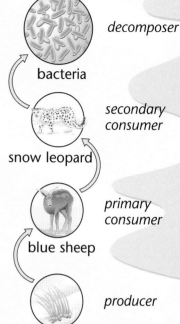

decomposer
bacteria

secondary consumer
snow leopard

primary consumer
blue sheep

producer
grass

Fungi

Fungi grow thin threads called hyphae through dead wood and other plant parts. The hyphae make chemicals that rot the waste around them. Then the fungi can take in some of the plants' nutrients. In some mountain habitats, mushrooms live among the piles of fallen leaves and needles under trees such as dwarf willows and pines.

Pine trees rely on fungi such as mushrooms to recycle nutrients from their dead needles.

Bacteria

Even in thin mountain soils, there are millions of tiny **bacteria** in the ground. Most of these bacteria live in thin films of water trapped around small bits, or particles, of soil. Some feed on chemicals, such as proteins, that are found in the bodies of living things. Others feed on the waste products of other bacteria.

Animals that help decomposers

When some animals eat dead **organisms** or animal waste, they help break them down into smaller bits that **decomposers** can use. These mini-**scavengers** include worms and insects such as maggots and beetles. Springtails are tiny insects that can survive under snow on mountaintops, where there is virtually nothing alive or growing. They survive by eating dead insects, **fungi**, and other waste that blows there on the wind.

Dung beetles lay eggs on animal droppings. The beetle **larvae** feed on these droppings, or dung, when they hatch. This breaks down the waste, making it easier for decomposers to use.

How Are Mountain Food Chains Different in Different Places?

Food chains can be very different from one mountain to another. Mountain food chains are affected by **climate**, the height of the mountain, and the amount of human activity in the area.

Mount Kenya

Mount Kenya is Africa's second highest mountain at around 17,060 feet (5,200 meters) high. On the lower slopes, the **producers** are rain forest trees, with areas of bamboo up higher. Near the top is open ground with fewer plants.

The **primary consumers** in the forests include elephants and bushbuck and bongo antelopes. All of these eat grass, leaves, and twigs. Black-and-white colobus monkeys also eat tree leaves. Hyraxes are small **herbivores** that climb up rocks using sticky pads on their feet. Olive baboons are **omnivores** that eat plants such as fruit, grass, and roots, as well as animal food such as insects and bird eggs. **Secondary consumers** include cats such as servals, which eat birds and hyrax. Larger cats, such as leopards, hunt larger **prey**, including bushbucks, colobus monkeys, and olive baboons.

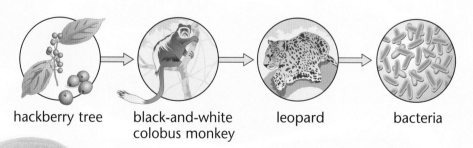

hackberry tree   black-and-white   leopard   bacteria
colobus monkey

This is just one of many Mount Kenya food chains.

The Alps

The Alps are a huge mountain range in Europe. The highest mountain is Mont Blanc at 15,770 feet (4,807 meters). High Alpine areas are made up of steep cliffs and fallen rocks with little plant life. Even so, there are many food chains here.

The chamois is a kind of goat that jumps from rock to rock on its hoofed feet. It feeds on patches of flowers, moss, and **lichen**. The lynx, a kind of wild cat, is one of its **predators**. Groups of marmots live underground in burrows and feed on grass. When marmots are feeding, one of them watches for predators such as **birds of prey**.

Griffon vultures and maggots are Alpine **scavengers**. They eat the flesh of dead animals, such as chamois, that they find on the slopes. **Bacteria** slowly break down any remains they leave behind.

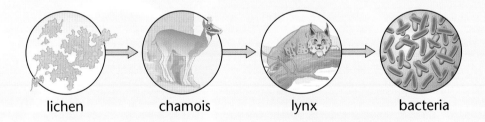

| lichen | chamois | lynx | bacteria |

*This shows a food chain in an Alpine mountain **habitat**.*

The Rocky Mountains

The Rocky Mountains run for almost 3,100 miles (5,000 kilometers) through North America, from Alaska to Mexico. Many different **primary consumers**, such as mountain goats and marmots, eat grasses and other small **producers** for much of the year. In autumn, **mammals** from small snowshoe hares to enormous moose, and birds such as grouse, feast on the small, **energy**-rich berries of shrubs such as mountain cranberry.

Bobcats and golden eagles are **secondary consumers** of snowshoe hares, marmots, and grouse. Some of the largest predators in the Rockies are **omnivores**. For example, black bears eat small **prey** such as marmots, fish, and insects, but also roots and berries.

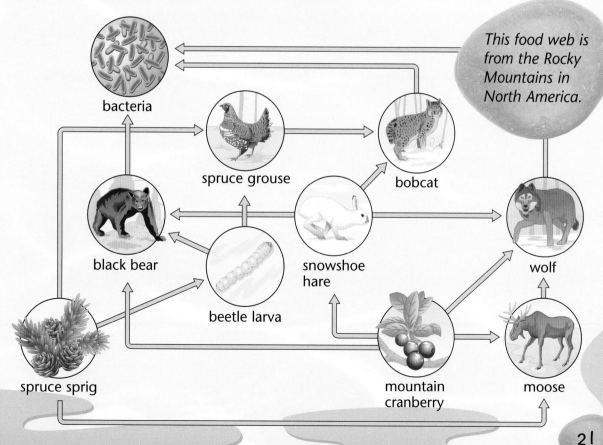

This food web is from the Rocky Mountains in North America.

bacteria

spruce grouse

bobcat

black bear

snowshoe hare

wolf

beetle larva

spruce sprig

mountain cranberry

moose

What Happens to a Food Web When a Food Chain Breaks Down?

Many mountain food chains and webs around the world are at risk because of human activities. When people affect a single link in a habitat's food chain, this can affect many other links of that food chain and the whole food web. The effects are much greater when whole areas of habitat are damaged.

Habitat destruction

Mountain forests are being cut down for their wood, as well as to clear land for farming and mining. Loss of mountain forests in northern Europe means there is little food and shelter for rare European bears. Miners in the Appalachians in the United States are destroying some mountains to get at the coal below. This process has destroyed large areas of forest that are home to birds such as water thrushes. People have also filled in or **polluted** mountain streams, killing fish, insects, and other animals.

Large areas of mountain forest in Oregon have been cut down for their wood.

This huge litter dump was made by tourists visiting Mount Sinai in Israel.

Cutting down mountain forests can lead to more problems. Trees stop soil and snow from slipping down steep mountain slopes. When there are fewer trees, there are more harmful landslides and avalanches.

Tourism

Visitors to mountain areas can sometimes be a good thing. They provide work for local people in businesses such as hotels. However, tourists may drop litter, pollute water, and use up firewood. Mountain walkers and climbers can wear away paths. Some people accidentally start fires that can destroy large areas of plants and small animals.

Acid rain

When people burn fuels, especially in factories or vehicle engines, polluting gases are released. These mix with rainwater to make acid rain. Acid rain damages mountain lakes, killing their fish. It also destroys leaves on trees, removing the **producer** link from many food chains.

The ice cliffs around Glacier Bay in Alaska are melting as a result of global warming.

Climate change

Scientists believe that the world's **climate** is changing. Power stations, factories, and cars have created a layer of **polluting** gases in the atmosphere that traps the Sun's heat. The resulting global rise in temperature affects mountains in different ways. For example, in the Rocky Mountains of Canada, beetles that eat pine leaves used to die out in cold winters. Warmer winters have allowed more beetles to survive, and they have killed huge areas of mountain forest.

Breaking the Chain: Unwanted Additions

Food chains can be broken if a new **organism** is introduced to a **habitat.** In New Zealand, people have brought new animals, such as dogs and ferrets, to the mountains where giant wetas—the world's heaviest insects—live. These giant wetas are now rare, mostly because many have been killed by these new animals.

How Can We Protect Mountain Food Chains?

Around the world, people are working to protect mountain habitats and the living things that make up mountain food chains and webs.

Scientists study mountain habitats to see how changes there affect plants and animals. For example, scientists studying Mount Kilimanjaro in Tanzania discovered that there is much less ice and snow at the top of the mountain than there used to be. With less snow to melt into water and flow into streams and rivers, mountain and river wildlife has been affected.

In the 1980s, scientists in the Himalayan Mountains found that the number of snow leopards was decreasing. People were illegally hunting both the snow leopards and animals such as antelope that the snow leopards usually use for food. The scientists encouraged the Chinese government to establish the Chang Tang Wildlife Preserve in Tibet in 1993 to protect these animals.

At the Chang Tang Wildlife Preserve in Tibet, scientists study how climate change is affecting the amount of snow on Mount Everest.

Conservation groups

Conservation groups are organizations that work to protect the natural world and the plants and animals that live in it. Many conservation groups are charities that raise money from ordinary people to fund their work. International conservation groups include the World Wildlife Fund and Friends of the Earth. They carry out research and work to make the public aware of issues such as the destruction of mountain **habitats** and the problems facing **endangered species**, including European wolves and the Iberian lynx.

Conservation groups also run projects to teach people living on or near mountains about how they can help to protect the habitat. For example, in the Himalayas, conservation groups are encouraging people not to cut down trees and shrubs to burn as fuel, but to cook with an oil called kerosene instead.

This conservationist is planting trees to help restore a mountain habitat.

Research a mountain food web

You can research your own mountain food chains and webs. You could use information from this and other books and from sources on the Internet. When you are working on your food chains, think about the factors that affect what lives there. For example, is the habitat hot or cold, wet or dry? Here are some other things to think about when making food chains.

1. What are the plant **producers** in the habitat?
2. What animals live there? Try to group animals that are similar, such as insects, birds, and **mammals**, for example.
3. What does each animal eat?
4. Which are the **predators** and which are the **prey**?
5. Link some of the different **organisms** together in food chains and then combine them in a food web.

If you visit a mountain, try to act in ways that protect the habitat for plants and animals. Stay on paths, to avoid wearing down the land or disturbing wildlife. This hiker is walking toward Mt. Ama Dablam in the Himalayas.

Where Are the World's Main Mountains?

The map on these pages shows you where some of the major mountain ranges in the world are located.

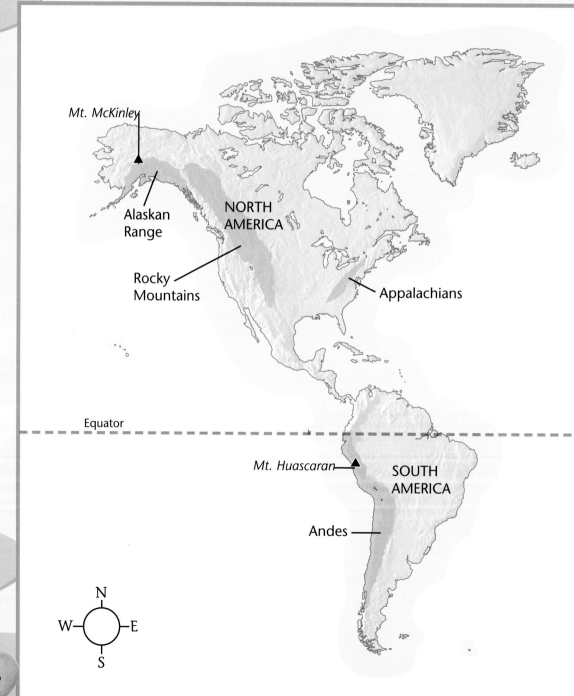

Mt. McKinley

Alaskan Range

NORTH AMERICA

Rocky Mountains

Appalachians

Equator

Mt. Huascaran

SOUTH AMERICA

Andes

N
W — E
S

ASIA

Caucasus
Mountains

EUROPE

Pyrenees

Alps

Himalayas

Atlas
Mountains

AFRICA

Ethiopian
Highlands

Mt. Kenya

Equator

Mt. Kilimanjaro

AUSTRALIA

Glossary

bacteria (singular bacterium) tiny living decomposers found everywhere

bird of prey bird that hunts animals for food

carnivore animal that eats the flesh of another animal

climate general conditions of weather in an area

consumer organism that eats other organisms

decomposer organism that breaks down and gets nutrients from dead plants and animals and their waste

endangered at risk of dying out completely, as a species of animal or plant

energy power to grow, move, and do things

fungi (singular fungus) group of decomposer organisms including mushrooms, toadstools, and their relatives

habitat place where an organism lives

herbivore animal that eats plants

hibernate to go into a special long sleep to avoid bad weather and scarce food

larvae (singular larva) young of some insects and other animals

lichen kind of low-growing organism made up of fungi and algae living together

mammal animal that feeds its babies on milk from its own body

nutrient chemical that plants and animals need to live

omnivore animal that eat both plants and other animals

organism living thing

photosynthesis process by which plants make their own food using carbon dioxide (a gas in the air), water, and energy from sunlight

pollen small grains that are the male parts of a flower. Pollen combines with eggs (female flower parts) to form seeds.

pollinator insect that carries pollen from the male part of a flower to the female part

pollution when chemicals or other substances that can damage animal or plant life escape into water, soil, or the air

predator animal that hunts and eats other animals

prey animal that is caught and eaten by a predator

primary consumer animal that eats plants

producer organism (plant) that can make its own food

rodent mammal with large gnawing front teeth, such as a mouse or rat

scavenger organism that feeds on dead plant and animal material and waste

secondary consumer animal that eats primary consumers and other secondary consumers

species group of organisms that are similar to each other and can breed together to produce young

temperate belonging to a region of
the world that has warm summers
and cold, wet winters

tree line height on a mountain
above which it is too cold and
windy for trees to grow

More Books to Read

Baldwin, Carol. *Living on a Mountain*. Chicago, IL: Heinemann, 2003.

Cheshire, Gerard. *Nature Unfolds Mountains and Deserts*. New York: Crabtree, 2002.

Lauber, Patricia. *Who Eats What?* New York: HarperCollins, 2001.

Llewellyn, Claire. *Animal Atlas*. Santa Monica, CA.: Creative Publishing, 2003.

Lovell, Scarlett, et al. *Exploring Mountain Habitats*. New York: Mondo Publishing, 1999.

Price, Martin. *Mountains*. Stillwater, MN.: Voyageur Press, 2002.

Royston, Angela. *Mountains*. Chicago, IL: Raintree, 2004.

Squire, Ann. *Animal Homes*. Danbury, CT.: Scholastic Library, 2002.

Index